Lord, Help Me Love My Sister

Lord, Help Me Love My Sister

"She breathed on my food again!"

Clair G. Cosby

HERALD PRESS
Scottdale, Pennsylvania
Kitchener, Ontario
1986

Library of Congress Cataloging in Publication Data

Cosby, Clair G., 1944-
  Lord, help me love my sister.

  Summary: A book of prayers for young girls between the ages of eight and fourteen who are trying to survive living with a sister and develop a special relationship for the years to come.
  1. Young women—Prayer-books and devotions—English. [1. Prayer books and devotions. 2. Sisters] I. Title.
  BV4551.2.C67   1986   242'.633   86-4831
  ISBN 0-8361-3413-3 (pbk.)

Scripture quotations are from *The New English Bible.*
© The Delegates of the Oxford University Press and the Syndics of the Cambridge University Press 1961, 1970. Reprinted by permission.

LORD, HELP ME LOVE MY SISTER
Copyright © 1986 by Herald Press, Scottdale, Pa. 15683
    Published simultaneously in Canada by Herald Press,
    Kitchener, Ont. N2G 4M5. All rights reserved.
Library of Congress Catalog Card Number: 86-4831
International Standard Book Number: 0-8361-3413-3
Printed in the United States of America
Design by Gwen Stamm/Cover photo by Gail S. Denham

91 90 89 88 87 86 10 9 8 7 6 5 4 3 2 1

*To my daughters
Sarah
and
Sallie.*

Contents

A Sister is a Special Gift 9

1 Corinthians 13:4-8a, 13............................... 13

She Borrowed My Purple Sweater Without Asking 16
She Has All the Neat Clothes and I Have to Wear Her
Hand-Me-Downs 17

She Runs Faster Than I Do 18
She's Never Afraid 19

She Really Cares When I Hurt 20
Please Heal Her Hand 21

She Breathed on My Food Again 22
She Takes Herself Too Seriously 23

She Won't Cooperate with Me 24
She's Always Trying to Tell Me What to Do 25

She Shared Her Room with Me Last Night 26
She Understands How I Feel 27

She Got to Sit in the Front Seat of the Car 28
She Gets SO Dramatic When She Doesn't Get Her Way .. 29

She Tries to Steal My Friends 30
She Won't Share Her Friends 31

She's Gone Visiting Our Grandparents 32
She Had to Stay Home This Time 33

She Calls Me an Idiot 34
She Makes Me Feel Like an Idiot 35

She Never Asks Permission	36
She's So Obedient She Makes Me Sick	37
She Really Liked Her Birthday Present	38
She Picked a Special Gift	39
She Has Memorized Her Times Tables	40
She Writes Stories for Fun	41
She Gets Rewarded for Not Biting Her Nails	42
She Thinks She's So Great	43
She Loaned Me Her Diary Key	44
She Can Open Her Bank Now	45
She Wants to Do What I'm Doing	46
She Always Gets to Do Things First	47
She Stamps Her Feet and Throws Tantrums	48
She Gets So Angry That She Frightens Me	49
She's Lost Her Purse	50
She's Really Trying to Help	51
She Doesn't Have to Set an Example	52
She Doesn't Have to Hear How Great Her Older Sister Is	53
She's So Cute and Cuddly	54
She's So Sweet and Huggy	55
Lord, Help Me Love My Sister	56
Lord, Help Me Love My Sister	57
Prayers for My Sister	59
The Author	75

A Sister Is a Special Gift

Last week as I was looking through a needlecraft magazine an embroidery kit caught my eye. A pastel heart was outlined with roses, daisies, and violets. In the center were the words: "A Sister Is a Forever Friend."

This beautiful picture and beautiful thought brought back memories of those times when I had wanted a sister. As a lonely little girl, I had thought it would be so much fun to share my life with a sister—to share a rainy afternoon, the boring backseat ride on vacations, the fears when my mother went to the hospital, the excitement of the first day back at school in the fall.

Now—although I still do not have a sister—I have two daughters with whom to share this happy thought: "A sister is a forever friend." But many times they don't seem to enjoy being sisters. They spend so many hours being upset or jealous or intolerant with each other. The years are passing, and half of their lives at home together are through, but they haven't fully learned to be friends.

How could the sister with whom you battle daily be your friend forever?

You share the same family and background. You are really more alike than you realize right now. You may have the same color hair or eyes, the same physical abilities, the same tilt to your head—or you may not. But you do have the same parents and grandparents, the same neighbors, pets, church, and school. You live in the same home, come from the same town, and go on the same vacations. Your grandma may even buy you the same dresses in different sizes!

Many of the problems that you face, much of the loneliness that you feel, the frustrations that come as you start to grow up are the same for you and your sister. And she will come to understand—maybe even better than your parents or best friend—your joys, your hurts, your growing pains.

As you grow older and memories are more important to you, your sister will remember as you do the birthday when you received a camera, the sunny afternoon when the family panned for emeralds in the mountains, your first piano recital. You will remember as she does the Christmas when you both received shiny new bicycles, her butterfly collection, her glittery sequin-covered party outfit.

Through the years you will share clothes, books, records, clubhouses, games, and parents. And, through this sharing time, will grow the bonds of a special friendship—close enough to last through those years away at college, dear enough to cover the miles when you live in Texas and she lives in California, strong enough to outlast the times when you are both too busy to do more than telephone or write a letter every month or so.

You will be forever friends—if you can just *survive* living together today!

Today is when she borrows your favorite purple sweater without asking or when you call her an idiot in exasperation. Today is when mother seems to love her more than you. Today you get to go to camp and leave her behind because you are two years older. How will both of you get through today and become really good friends tomorrow?

I believe that God wants us to love each other within our families. I also believe that God will help us to learn to love each other better, if we ask him to help. I believe that we should talk to God about our problems with other people, even our own family. We should ask God's help in making hard situations easier, difficult days more peaceful, sharing more natural, and sisters more loving.

Any two people who live closely together will at times misunderstand one another, be hurt by little words and actions, or even may become angry with someone else and take it out on each other. But with God's help people also learn to forgive, to wait, to listen, to share.

This book is a collection of prayers asking God's help in difficulties between sisters. As you read these prayers, think about yourself and your sister. Do they fit you two?

Write your own prayers, about problems between you and your sister, on the blank pages at the back of this book.

Remember, whatever it is that is keeping you unhappy with each other today—you can talk about it with God. Ask for his help.

God has given you a special gift—a sister—and he wants you two to be forever friends.

—Clair G. Cosby
Warrenton, Virginia

Love is patient; love is kind and envies no one.

Love is never boastful, nor conceited, nor rude; never selfish, not quick to take offence. Love keeps no score of wrongs; does not gloat over [my sister's] sins, but delights in the truth.

There is nothing love cannot face; there is no limit to its faith, its hope, and its endurance.

Love will never come to an end. . . . In a word, there are three things that last for ever: faith, hope, and love; but the greatest of them all is love.

—1 Corinthians 13:4-8a; 13

Lord, Help Me Love My Sister

Lord, She Borrowed My Purple Sweater Without Asking

Almost every day while we are dressing for school she comes down the hall to my room to look over what is hanging in my closet. She just walks in. She doesn't knock. She doesn't even say anything to me. She just starts going through my closet as if my clothes were hers.

I wish that we couldn't wear the same size. I wish that she were a foot shorter than me and that everything I own was way too big for her.

My clothes are my own, and that purple sweater is my favorite one. I can remember the windy January day when I came home from school feeling depressed because I had so much homework that night. My parents had been out shopping, and Mom had bought me the purple sweater because she knew that it was my favorite color. Just running my hand over the soft yarn made me feel special and loved.

There are some things that I wouldn't mind sharing, but my sister seems to know just what clothes I want for my very own. Then she chooses those and makes my parents think I'm selfish when I refuse to let her wear them.

Lord, help me to learn to share my clothes more willingly with my sister, and help her to learn there are some special belongings we shouldn't ask each other to share.

Lord, She Has All the Neat Clothes and I Have to Wear Her Hand-Me-Downs

I lay out my clothes at bedtime and then in the morning when I am dressing for school I start thinking about how my sister has most of the new clothes. Hers are always the latest style. Hers are in the popular colors. My friends have already seen all of my clothes—last year on my sister!

I wish she would share her new clothes with me more willingly now that we are almost the same size. Sometimes I go to her closet before school and just think about how many clothes she has to choose from.

My clothes are alright. Well, really they are fine—it's just that I don't get too many special things bought just for me. It's hard not to feel like my parents love her more than me when I have spent most of my life in her hand-me-downs.

Mom says that by wearing my sister's outgrown things I have more to choose from. Mom says she still buys me a few outfits each season and that each of us gets new clothes when we *need* them. I know she's right, but it still bothers me.

Lord, help me learn not to be jealous of my sister's clothes and help her to understand how I feel and sometimes offer to share her new clothes with me.

Lord, She Runs Faster Than I Do

She runs faster. She swims across the pool before me. She roller skates more smoothly. Every time we ride bikes or throw balls or play tag, my little sister makes me feel physically inferior.

Why is her body stronger than mine? Why couldn't I be just as well coordinated? Why does she sail so easily through school physical fitness tests that are always so hard for me?

I wish that I were more like my sister. I get embarrassed when I'm slower running the bases than my classmates, when I miss an easy catch, when I'm not picked first to play on a team.

SHE IS!

Her favorite things are aerobics and gymnastics—and oh, she does run fast. Sometimes I see her racing across the backyard with her hair blowing back from her face, and I can't believe she is my sister . . . and I wonder what is wrong with me.

Lord, give me the strength and determination to learn to run a little faster, and help me accept the differences between my sister and me.

Lord, She's Never Afraid

She sleeps without a light on in her room. She goes tent camping in the middle of the woods. She stands up in front of the whole school to introduce a special program. Every time we are in a new situation, facing new people, unsure of what is going on, my big sister makes me feel bashful, frightened, and inferior.

Why is she so confident? Why couldn't I stand up on the stage and speak without my shoulders twisting and turning and my mouth going dry? Why does she seem so at home at club meetings and dinners in fancy restaurants and making those oral school reports that are so hard for me?

I wish I were more like my sister. I get embarrassed when my teachers and classmates realize that I shouldn't be the one picked to do a part in the spring play, when I dissolve into giggles in the middle of a memorized poem, when my hands get fidgety.

HERS DON'T!

Her favorite things are drama club and choir performances and meeting new people—and she does it so well. Sometimes I see her talking across the room with two or three adults, looking grown up and confident, and I can't believe she is my sister . . . and I wonder what is wrong with me.

Lord, give me the courage to overcome my fears and help me accept the differences between my sister and me.

Lord, She Really Cares When I Hurt

I did the dumbest thing today at school. I was walking along a pipe on the school yard—balancing about six inches off the ground—and, somehow, I slipped. It seems impossible, but I've broken my hand. Only *I* could do that! I wasn't even doing anything dangerous or daring—and I broke my hand. I really felt foolish.

By the time I got on the school bus, my hand had started to swell. My sister saw it was hurt, and she kept asking me how I felt. She carried my books to the house and called for Mom to come. She ran to the refrigerator for some ice before she even took her coat off.

Now my hand is throbbing and aching, and I'll probably miss school tomorrow. I feel so clumsy. The doctor put a cast on my hand and arm. How will I practice piano?

My sister came to my room before she went to bed to ask me how I felt. She said she was sorry that I'd broken my hand. She really cares when I hurt.

Lord, sometimes it seems like she doesn't care about me at all. Thank you for helping her show me today that she loves me.

Lord, Please Heal Her Hand

When my sister got on the school bus today, I could tell right away that something was wrong. She looked worried-sad, and she wasn't talking. Then I saw that her hand was big, really big. She broke it at school. She didn't know how badly it was hurt, so she hadn't told the teacher.

The doctor put a cast on her hand this afternoon, but it still felt bad at bedtime. Mom says my sister will need help dressing and carrying things for several weeks. That will really bother her because she likes to do things for herself. My sister is very independent.

Sometimes people have broken hands that don't heal right. Some people can't ever play the piano or hold a pencil like everyone else. I hope she hasn't thought about that. She would really be upset if she did.

Lord, please heal my sister's hand so that she can use it like she always did, and please tell me what I can do to help her while she's hurting.

Lord, She Breathed on My Food Again

Everyone had filled their plates at supper. Mom and Dad were talking about the garden. And I don't know what my little brother was doing. But all at once I saw my sister leaning over the table, and I knew it was coming. Before I could do anything about it, she *breathed* on my food.

She knows that bothers me. It makes me feel sick to think of all of her germs getting all over my food. She does it just to tease me. After she had done it tonight she just sat there quietly grinning while I screamed, "She's breathed on my food!"

My parents don't know how much it bothers me. I wish I didn't react so much. That's just what she wants. She really *wants* me to make a scene and get all upset and make Mom and Dad think I'm being foolish.

Some nights I don't even want to go to the dinner table at all because I know, sometime during the meal, she'll manage to act like she has something to tell me. She'll lean up close, and—quicker than I can move the plate away—she'll do it again.

Lord, help me not to be so bothered when she breathes on my food, and help her to realize that what she started as a joke never was at all funny to me.

Lord, She Takes Herself Too Seriously

I breathed on her food at dinner tonight, and you would have thought I'd poured poison over the mashed potatoes. It doesn't take much to set her off yelling and swinging her arms and threatening to take me apart. All I really have to do is twist around in my chair and start to lean towards her plate. Sometimes I don't even have to actually breathe on her food. She is waiting for it, and so she figures I've done it before I even get a good mouthful of air.

I guess that I shouldn't tease her so much, but, honestly, she takes herself so seriously that she doesn't see the humor in *anything*.

I mean, we all make mistakes. We say things wrong, or fall over our own feet, or drop a glassful of water. It seems to me, we should just laugh, clean up the mess, and get on with things.

But MY sister? No, indeed! When she makes a silly mistake, she tries to cover it up, or starts feeling guilty, or starts worrying about what people will think of her.

If she could just see how she looked tonight at the dinner table. But maybe my teasing isn't changing her at all.

Lord, forgive me if I've really hurt my sister, and help me not to tease her so much.

Lord, She Won't Cooperate with Me

It happens every day. It happens while we are playing a game, when we are getting into the car, when Mother asks us to get something from the basement. My sister will not cooperate with me!

I am beginning to think that it wouldn't matter if I suggested doing her favorite craft, eating her favorite food, or watching her favorite program. Just because I suggest something, she thinks it isn't a good idea.

We are supposed to be sisters and get along together. We are supposed to do some things together. When are we ever going to learn if we don't start working together now?

It usually winds up that I give in and do what she wants to do so that there won't be a big fight. My parents expect me to be more mature and to make compromises. But it isn't fair. Why should I always be the one to give in? Am I supposed to grow up always giving in because I'm older?

Well, I won't! She has to learn to cooperate with *me*. My ideas are just as good as hers, and I am older, and I have had more experience than she has. Sometimes we should play by MY rules or listen to MY record, or ride bikes where *I* want to ride.

Lord, help me to stand up for my own ideas when I feel they are important and help me to teach my sister to cooperate by not always giving in to her.

Lord, She's Always Trying to Tell Me What to Do

Maybe it's because she's older than I am or maybe it's just the way she is, but every day she tries to tell me how to do things. She figures that she has all the right answers, and she isn't willing for me to find things out on my own.

When Mother tells us to load the dishwasher, my sister tells me how to put the glasses in. When Dad asks me to find him a screwdriver from the garage, my sister tells me where she thinks it is. When I pick a TV show, my sister tells me she doesn't think I should watch it.

Who does she think she is?

It isn't fair just because she was born a couple of years before me that she should run my whole life and make all of my decisions for me. I will not let her do it! There are things I must decide and try for myself.

Maybe she does it out of love; maybe she wants me to learn from her own mistakes. But somehow I must learn to stand up for myself and discover who *I* am, and what *I* think, and how *I* will act.

Lord, help me to stand up for my own ideas when I feel they are important and help me to teach my sister to cooperate by not always giving in to her.

Lord, She Shared Her Room with Me Last Night

Our aunt and uncle are visiting for the weekend, and guests always use my room. My sister's room has twin beds, so we usually sleep together when there is company. Sometimes my sister doesn't want me to stay in her room. Sometimes she piles books and clothes on the bed I'm supposed to sleep on. But last night she made space for me without my asking.

It was nice to slide down under the sheet and blanket and lie there listening and talking in the half-darkened room. She told me how she felt about going to camp this summer for the first time. She told me how excited she is about being able to ride the horses and how worried she is about being in the cabins at night.

I really felt good that we could lie there and talk like best friends. I think I made her feel better about camp when I shared how at first I had been afraid last year too—but how much fun I had once we started hiking and swimming.

Lord, thank you for giving us a good sharing time together last night, and please help my sister not to worry about camp.

Lord, She Understands How I Feel

My sister slept on the other twin bed in my room last night because we had company. When Mom sent us to bed, we didn't go right to sleep. I was lying there thinking my sister must believe I'm a baby to want a night-light beside my bed. I started thinking how dark it will be in the middle of the woods at night when we go to camp this summer. I asked my sister what camp was really like.

She told me about the things she did at camp last year and then—how did she know?—she asked me how I felt about going. And she listened while I talked.

She shared with me how afraid she had been on the ride to camp last year, how much she had wanted to go back home with Dad when he left her there. I never knew she was ever afraid of anything. It made me feel better to know that she understands how I feel. I really want to go to camp, but I'm a little worried about it too.

I'm glad she shared with me last night. I'm glad she'll be at camp when I go this summer. It's good to have a friend you can talk to.

Thank you, Lord, for helping my sister tell me she was afraid about camp last year, and please help us be better friends.

Lord, She Got to Sit in the Front Seat of the Car

We were riding home from a picnic with family friends yesterday, and my sister asked if she could sit in the front seat of the car. She always asks if she can—when we go shopping, or on a ride, or on a trip—she always wants to sit up front between my Mom and Dad.

Most of the time they say yes to her. She just climbs over the seat and settles down, and Mom puts her arm around her—and my sister feels loved.

When I ask to sit up front, Mom says, "You've gotten so tall that you take up too much room," or "We're going through heavy traffic, and we don't want to be crowded," or "Your legs are so long! Where would we fit you?"

It just isn't fair. Sometimes I would like to get to sit there between my parents! If I can't, why should she?

I can't wait till my sister grows a few more inches, and they think she's too big too!

Lord, it just isn't fair to have to grow up. I miss leaning up against Mom on a car trip and feeling drowsy and cuddled and loved.

Lord, She Gets SO Dramatic When She Doesn't Get Her Way

My sister got angry again yesterday when I asked to sit up front in the car. She doesn't think it's fair for me to get to sit up front if she can't. She thinks I'm taking our parents' love from her.

She gripes and leans over the back of the seat and then starts moping about it all.

At least she had Mom and Dad for two years alone before I was born. She got to be an only child. She could do things just with them. She was the special one!

I've always had to share my parents. I wasn't here until after my sister, and I was so little that I can't remember what it was like before my brother was born. I'm just in the middle—never the oldest so I can do things first, never the youngest so I get rocked to sleep or extra bedtime stories.

So I ask to sit between our parents on rides—and it feels good when they say I can. I hope I never get too big to sit up front.

Lord, it just isn't fair to always be the middle one. I never was "only" or special. I don't care if it makes my sister mad when I get my way.

Lord, She Tries to Steal My Friends

My best friend is in a different classroom this year—so we have to talk on the phone after school or get together sometimes on the weekends.

We've been friends for two years now. We both came to our school new, and we were in the same classroom twice. We really are a lot alike. It's good to have a friend who is studying the same things, likes the same things, and can share your secrets.

So, what happens when my best friend comes over to spend a Saturday? My sister tries to butt in. *She* goes to the door with me to greet my friend, walks back to my room with us, sits on the bed. She's just always hanging around.

Oh, I wouldn't mind if we spent a little time together, all three of us, but I don't get much privacy to talk with my friend even when Mom tells my sister to let us alone. My sister is always sort of nearby—waiting for us to open the door or walk out of the room.

I really look forward to those days when my friend is coming to visit. I plan the things we will do. I think about showing her my newest clothes or playing a record together. But it seems like the day is gone before we get to do half of the things I wanted to, because we had to spend so much of the time with my nosy sister.

Lord, help my sister see that I need other friends besides her and that there are times when my friends and I want to be alone.

Lord, She Won't Share Her Friends

My sister's best friend came over to spend the day, and you would have thought I had the plague. From the moment her friend's mother pulled into the driveway, my sister was pushing me out of the way. I was expected to sink into the floor or disappear into the air. I wasn't to talk to them or play with them or be in the same part of the house as they were.

I don't see why they couldn't *willingly* spend a little of their time with me. I mean, I'm good enough to play with when no one else is around. Then my sister wants me to play a game, or put a puzzle together, or trade stickers, or go climb a tree with her.

But when she can have someone else here, it's goodbye sister, hello friend.

Actually, my sister's best friend is not all that much like her. She has a lot in common with me too. I mean we could be friends just as much as she and my sister could.

I don't want to steal her friend. I just want to be noticed and accepted. Then maybe I'd be bored with what they want to do, and I'd go do my things without them.

Lord, help my sister to see that I don't like being dropped like a worn-out toy whenever someone else is available. Help her to share her friends, and help me to be the kind of friend they want to share with.

Lord, She's Gone Visiting Our Grandparents

I was really glad to see her go. I smiled to myself as she made a big deal of having the right clothes to put in her suitcase, and spending money, and a book—and on, and on, and on.

I thought it would be good to have one less child around to share my parents with, my friends with, my time with.

I thought that now I wouldn't have to whisper when I talked on the phone, wondering if she were in the kitchen trying to listen.

But, I miss her.

It just isn't the same to have her room empty down the hall. It's really quiet here. And there isn't really anyone to talk with—I mean, my brother is just too little, and my parents aren't the same as a sister.

Sometimes she helps me decide which skirt to wear or whether I should part my hair on the side or in the middle. Sometimes we sit downstairs and watch TV or go outside to collect wild flowers to press and make bookmarks.

She really knows a lot about things. We spend a lot of time together. The days seem sort of long without her.

Lord, I miss my sister. Help us to get along better when she comes home. Help her to miss me too.

Lord, She Had to Stay Home This Time

I love going away from home. My grandma and granddad let each of us visit four or five days each summer *alone*. It's terrific!

They take me to get my hair done and out to eat, and we always go sightseeing some place special. Granddad talks with me like I'm grown up, and Grandma cooks my favorite foods. They make me feel that I am really special. I love to go.

But it's lonesome here without my sister.

Everybody thinks we fight all the time, that we don't like being together and don't know how to enjoy each other's company.

But, we do.

My sister and I have long talks while we are climbing the magnolia tree or resting on the curb on a break from bike riding. She helps me think of crafts to do or tells me about books she's read that she knows I'll like. We dream about what we'll do when we grow up. We try to understand what our parents are planning and thinking too.

It's really great to be so special away from home. But it's lonesome too—I mean, who is there to tell about the ponies I saw on the way out to dinner, or to show my new hairstyle to, or to play that new game with?

Lord, I miss my sister. Help us to get along better when I go home. Help her to miss me too.

Lord, She Calls Me an Idiot

It doesn't come at any one time or any regular situation. We could be in the middle of a game or trading stickers or dressing for school. She'll get angry and scream, "You *idiot.*"

My parents don't want her to do it. They tell her not to. Sometimes they punish her for saying it. Sometimes they don't even know she has, because they aren't around to hear.

But she still says it.

And it makes me feel so bad.

I mean, I know I'm smart. I know I make good grades in school and the teachers like to call on me because I think of the answers to their questions. But there are so many times when I know I do dumb things, when the other kids don't accept me, when I drop something, or forget something really simple.

I know I'm smart—but sometimes I think to myself, "You idiot."

I don't want to have my sister calling me one. That just makes all of those feelings I am having about myself worse—like maybe she sees something I've missed and I'm even dumber than I thought.

Lord, please make my sister stop calling me names. Help her to see that it hurts deep down inside where I'm trying to feel better about myself.

Lord, She Makes Me Feel Like an Idiot

She picked out a game to play that had questions and answers. I just didn't know the answers, and I hate playing games like that. They really make me feel dumb—and they make me feel like everyone around the table is discovering how dumb I really am.

If they didn't know before, if they hadn't guessed what an idiot I am—they sure know now.

But my sister gets all of the questions right. It seems so easy for her, and she smiles and acts so relaxed and wants to keep on playing when I want to stop because I can't get any of the answers right.

She does it mostly in games. But there are times, too, when we are eating supper or at Grandma's or out shopping when something comes up—a new word or a place or a name from the news—that she knows, but I don't. Then she acts like *everyone* should know all about it—and she's done it again. I feel like an idiot.

Lord, please help my sister to learn how to tell me things without acting like I'm too dumb to know them. Help her to see that deep down inside I want to feel good about myself.

Lord, She Never Asks Permission

Sometimes I wish I had her kind of nerve. I mean, she never waits to see whether Mom and Dad will allow her to do something. She just does it.

She goes to the refrigerator and makes a snack; she goes into Mom's craft closet and finds material and pipe cleaners; she gets a hammer and nails from Dad's workbench and starts building a birdhouse. And most of the time she gets away with whatever it is she starts.

I think about making doll clothes and ask Mom for fabric. She says, "It's a little late at night to start a project like that." I design a car ramp for my brother's racer, ask Dad about some plywood I saw in the basement, and he says, "I was saving that for shelves beside the freezer." I ask Mom about getting some cookies from the cabinet, and she says, "Those are for the picnic tomorrow. How about an apple?"

Sometimes my sister gets into trouble for using something that was supposed to be for something else. But most of the time when she does it, they change *their* plans and think how independent and creative *she* is!

It really burns me up.

Lord, I want to be more independent. I want to start carrying out some of my plans and then seeing what happens. Help me to start doing more on my own.

Lord, She's So Obedient She Makes Me Sick

My sister would never dream of mixing up some sugar, wheat germ, a little butter, and an egg as a surprise dessert for the family. She would ask Mom if she had something planned and then ask permission to use the ingredients.

My sister would never dream of going to the garden to pick tomatoes and okra. She wouldn't want to upset Dad by bringing in vegetables that weren't ready.

My sister wouldn't dream of refusing to read to our little brother even when she would rather read one of her own mysteries.

I haven't decided if she's really good and obedient or if it is some plot to make me look worse when I get into trouble for going ahead and doing things before asking.

Oh, I do get in trouble every once in a while. Mom was not at all happy when I cut a circle out of some red cloth she was planning to use last Christmas. And Dad really got on me for sawing a 2×4 in half that he had bought for building shelves.

I just start thinking about what I want to make or do, and I forget to ask permission. SHE never forgets.

They think she's so good and obedient, but I think I get to do more things. Parents seem to have an automatic tape that says no when you ask them about using their things to start a project—so, sometimes it's better not to ask.

Lord, I wish my sister wouldn't be quite so obedient. It sometimes makes it very difficult around here.

Lord, She Really Liked Her Birthday Present

I had been thinking for a couple of months what she would like for her birthday. She likes lots of different things, but she has lots of things, too—and I wanted to give her something she would especially like.

I guess her favorite hobby is collecting stickers. She collects shells, stamps, and postcards, too, and has so many dolls that I don't see how she keeps all their clothes straight. And then there are the figures of horses that she has on her bookshelf—and she likes purses, too.

So there was a lot to choose from, but I thought she would like a box full of stickers.

It was fun to go to the gift shop and pick out the ones I thought she would like from rows full of rolls of stickers. Mom let me take a long time deciding, and she kept track of how much money I was spending. I enjoyed seeing how full the box was of stickers before I wrapped my sister's present.

She couldn't guess what I was giving her. She really was curious—and surprised.

She's in her room now putting them in her sticker album.

Lord, thank you for helping me to think of a gift that my sister really liked. I'm glad she is so happy today.

Lord, She Picked a Special Gift

My sister and I both have sticker collections. I guess most girls do. Mom lets us buy stickers with our allowance, as long as we don't spend all of our money on them.

There are so many stickers to choose from, and each one is special in a different way: some smell good, some are really beautiful, some shine, some are funny, some have textures, some are cute.

My sister and I sometimes go to the gift shop when Mom takes us to the mall. We look and talk together about the new stickers. I didn't know my sister was listening so closely to the ones I like.

I was really surprised that she gave me a boxful of most of the stickers I had been saving for. She picked a few new ones, too—ones I hadn't seen.

I've never had so many stickers at once. It's terrific! She's great for thinking of such a neat birthday present.

Lord, thank you for a sister who really tries to think of something special for my birthday. She does care about me.

Lord, She Has Memorized Her Times Tables

Mom was working on some kind of shopping list or something and just asked, "What's 6 times 8?" Before I could even think of the numbers my sister answered, "Forty-eight."

She didn't have to think; it just came out.

I was so embarrassed.

No one else seemed to notice that my little sister, two years younger than me, knows her multiplication tables better than I do!

I know most of them. It's just so boring sitting down and drilling $7 \times 4 = 28, 7 \times 5 = 35, 7 \times 6 = 42, 7 \times 7 = 49$. There are so many more interesting facts to learn.

But I've got to practice them, because there are four or five that I have to think about every time—and my sister knows them without thinking at all.

She didn't even realize that I didn't know the answer. At least that's one thing she can't tease me about.

Lord, help me to make myself sit down and learn those times tables, and help me not to be jealous because my sister already knows them.

Lord, She Writes Stories for Fun

She just thinks of things and writes them down and copies them over—and there's one more story! She has a whole collection of them. She's even started writing a teenage spy novel—just for fun.

I can't believe it.

Here I am sitting in my room trying to think of ten sentences to go with spelling words, going through torture. I can't wait to finish—and she's done with her homework and writing a story *for fun!*

It's so boring thinking of ten different sentences about silly words that I probably won't use in a year anyway. I can think of a hundred things I would rather be doing.

I have to think and think and think to come up with a sentence that doesn't sound like it was written by a six year old.

Nobody realizes how much I hate writing spelling sentences. I hope my sister doesn't find out. She'd probably come to my room and hang over me and give me a whole bunch of advice.

Lord, help me make myself settle down and write these sentences, and help me not to be jealous because my sister writes so easily.

Lord, She Gets Rewarded for Not Biting Her Nails

I can't believe it!

My mother has just promised my sister a dollar for every fingernail she doesn't bite for two months.

I can't believe it!

That's bribery. It's unfair! There is no way in this world that I would be given a chance to earn money for not biting my nails. If I had known there was such a profit in it, I would have bitten mine down to the quick ages ago.

Where's the reward for remembering to brush your teeth or wash your hands or eat with a fork or get up on time for school? It makes me sick that they are making such a big deal and giving her *ten* dollars because of a *bad* habit.

She'll hold out and get the money and then just throw it away on junk. If they gave me ten dollars, I'd put it in the bank. But I don't hear anyone offering me rewards.

Lord, I can't believe it. What has come over my parents? It seems so unfair that they reward the person with bad habits and ignore the person with good ones.

Lord, She Thinks She's So Great

She doesn't have a hard time with bad habits! She doesn't ever even think about biting her fingernails. She doesn't understand how hard it is to stop. She hasn't ever been reading a book and suddenly realized she's bitten her longest fingernail down to the quick again.

My sister is muttering all over the house about how unfair it is that my parents have offered me money to keep from biting my nails. She acts like they've just handed me a ten dollar bill and there's no work involved.

I don't even know if I *can* stop.

Biting my nails is something I just do. I don't even think about it. I don't know why I started or when I started.

I want to stop.

My fingers look so ugly. I don't like the kids at school to see my hands because they'll think they're yucky.

I wish I could stop.

Lord, help me stop biting my fingernails, and make my sister quit acting like it's all a game to me. I can't stop unless you help me.

Lord, She Loaned Me Her Diary Key

I can remember when she was given a diary for her birthday. My sister made such a *big deal* of hiding the key. Sometimes she would lose it because she had tried to hide it and the key had slipped into a crack or behind some boxes. She was so afraid that one of us would read her diary.

Now today she's loaned me the key.

We were cleaning our bedrooms this morning, and I found an old silver bank I've had since I was a baby. We lost the key to it years ago in one of our moves to a new house, so the bank was in a box in the closet.

I showed the bank to my sister, and she thought maybe her diary key would fit. It did. We were really surprised.

We didn't have time to look at all of the coins in the bank, but we're going to later, and she's left her key with me.

It feels good to know that she trusts me not to go down to her room and look in her diary.

Thank you, Lord, for helping my sister trust me.

Lord, She Can Open Her Bank Now

My sister has had a silver bank since she was a baby, but she couldn't open it because the key was lost. When I looked at the lock this morning, I tried to think of all the little keys I'd seen lately, and I remembered my diary.

Who would have thought that a diary key would fit a bank?

But it did!

We were both excited that the key worked. We want to check the coins carefully after we finish cleaning our rooms because she has an old coin collection.

I left my key with my sister.

It felt so good to be able to help her today. When we help each other, that's when we feel most like friends.

Thank you, Lord, for helping me think of my diary key when we were trying to open my sister's bank.

Lord, She Wants to Do What I'm Doing

If I get a camera for my birthday, she wants one too.
If I get a tape recorder for Christmas, she wants one too.

If I have a slumber party, she wants one too.

If I start taking piano lessons, she wants to too.

It almost seems like if I got a broken leg, she would want one just because I had one. Well, maybe that sounds ridiculous, but you know what I mean.

My parents have made me wait for certain things until I was old enough to appreciate them, or to take care of them, or to spend time practicing. My sister doesn't want to wait.

In fact, lots of times she wheedles and begs until my parents give in and let her have or do the thing earlier than I was allowed.

That's when I get mad about it!

I had to wait, and she doesn't—well, not always.

Lord, help her see that some things aren't as much fun if you get them too early, and help me not to get so angry when she doesn't have to wait.

Lord, She Always Gets to Do Things First

She's so lucky—I mean, she didn't have to be born first. It could have been me.

It's so hard to see her get to go to aerobics class, or piano lessons, or to computer camp and know that I have to wait. I'm the one too young for choir. I'm the one too young to wear hose or too "immature" to take care of a good camera.

When I see her having and doing things that I want to have and do, I get so discouraged. Do I really have to wait two more YEARS? Years take so long.

I'd love to be the first one to take cello lessons or become a cheerleader. I'd love to wear the first high heels or have the first baby-sitting job.

But, I'll always be second to her.

Doesn't she know how it feels to *know* you're second?

She doesn't like my asking Mom and Dad for the things she has. But she already has them, so why should she care? I'm still getting them second.

Lord, it's hard always to be second. Help me not to feel so jealous when my sister gets to be first.

Lord, She Stamps Her Feet and Throws Tantrums

Everyone in the house can tell when my sister is upset about something. Let me say it a little differently: everyone in the *neighborhood* can tell when my sister is angry.

She is a noisy person most of the time anyway. But when she is angry, look out!

She screams, pushes people and things that are in her way, slams her bedroom door, and—sometimes—lies on the bed kicking and pounding the pillow.

I stay away from her when she's angry, but I worry about her too.

It seems like she's out of control. It's almost like she can't get back into control until all of that energy is let loose.

Lord, it must frighten her to get so angry. Please help my sister to work out her anger without losing control of herself.

Lord, She Gets So Angry That She Frightens Me

Sometimes I push my sister too far. You know that I am trying to work on that, but sometimes I really make her angry.

Now, when *I* get angry, I get loud. When my sister gets angry, you can see her face and shoulders get stiff. She talks in a very soft voice and curls both of her hands into fists.

It frightens me because it's so unnatural.

She's *so* controlled.

I keep wondering what will happen one day when all of that control snaps. She could go crazy.

I stay away from my sister when she starts looking angry. I can tell when she's had enough teasing or when I've borrowed one too many things without asking, or when I've yelled the wrong thing at her.

She says, in a growling whisper with a murderous look on her face, "I could kill you.... I hate you.... I wish you were dead."

Lord, I know that she's usually a good and loving person, and I don't think she would really hurt me—but sometimes my sister frightens me.

Lord, She's Lost Her Purse

She didn't want anyone to know. She hasn't told Mom and Dad because they would just start telling her to be more responsible, or that she would find it if she would ever clean out her bedroom closet.

I can tell when my sister is worried about something.

She asked me this morning—very casually—if I had seen her purse.

Finally, she admitted that she hasn't been able to find it all week, and she had eight dollars in it.

We cleaned the basement family room today after school, but we didn't find her purse. We're going to pull everything out of her closet tomorrow if we can't find it anywhere else in the house.

Mom won't believe all this cleaning. She'll probably figure something is up soon.

Lord, please help my sister think of where she left her purse. She is worried, and I know you can help her.

Lord, She's Really Trying to Help

I know she thinks I'm silly not to tell Mom and Dad that I've lost my purse. I know that she would tell them if it were her, but she hasn't acted superior or bossy about this even once.

She's just pitched in and helped me look for it.

She started to pick up things in the family room in case it was under some books or puzzles or behind a chair. She looked in my brother's favorite hiding places just in case he's pulling tricks on me. She has even offered to help me clean out my bedroom closet—a real disaster area—tomorrow after school.

Not once has she given me her *opinions* on the matter. That means a lot, because I'm already feeling dumb for having lost my purse.

I mean, how many places can a purse be in a house? It's not *that* small. I really cannot believe I've lost it.

Lord, thank you for a sister who is willing to help even when I've done something stupid. Please help us find that purse.

Lord, She Doesn't Have to Set an Example

It seems like all of my life people have been telling me, "You shouldn't be so rowdy (or loud, or angry, or wasteful, or anything else they can think of). You have to set an example for your little sister and brother."

You know, sometimes I've wished I would be allowed to run a little freer.

Oh, I wouldn't do anything too wild. It's just that I feel I've always had the responsibility around my neck to be a little more grown up, a little more mature, a little more acceptable than my sister.

I'm to "set the example."

Most of the time I think she resents the example I set. She doesn't realize that it takes effort not to run down the hall, not to take the biggest piece of cake, not to talk back to a rude adult.

Sometimes I'd like to turn around and yell, "Well, I'm tired of setting the example. Let me make some big mistakes. Let me shout and run. Let me—"

But they never will allow me to do that now. They'd wonder why all at once I got rebellious.

Lord, I know I'm supposed to set a good example. Please help me not to feel so bound by my responsibility.

Lord, She Doesn't Have to Hear How Great Her Older Sister Is

It's like a curse!

It wouldn't matter if I were as smart as Einstein, as funny as a TV comedian, as beautiful as Miss America, as holy as a minister—I still wouldn't be as good as my big sister.

She's a paragon of virtue!

I dread the beginning of a school year until I find out if my teacher is one she had before. It's happened twice. They have had my dear sister years ago, and all of the great and wonderful things that she has done in the past have grown in their minds until there is just no way I can compete.

I know we aren't supposed to be in competition. After all, she's two years older than I am. But in real life people *do* make comparisons between us—it seems like every day.

We are different.

My sister would tell you that. We couldn't think and act alike if we tried. But she sure is a hard act to follow, and it seems like I don't come up to her example no matter how hard I try.

Lord, please let people see me as my own person. Help them to judge me by myself instead of as a poor copy of my sister.

Lord, She's So Cute and Cuddly

She has been ever since I can remember—blonde curly hair, bouncing around with a smile and a giggle. All of our family has reached out to cuddle her since she first started toddling around. She's adorable.

It makes me sick.

You can always tell when my sister is in the house. You can hear her laughing or singing. She seems to be all over the place—never anywhere for long.

Sometimes when I awake in the morning, she's already in the living room cuddled up on Mom's lap, talking, and feeling loved.

At her age, it makes me sick.

She does cute things. You have to smile at some of the stories she tells, and songs she sings, and faces she makes.

Lord, it's hard to have a sister who's so cute and cuddly. Everyone notices her instead of me.

Lord, She's So Sweet and Huggy

She's the dearest girl, so nice and polite, so sweet, so obedient. She wouldn't dream of being rowdy and loud. All of our relatives are proud of the way she acts, the perfect little lady.

It makes me sick.

She's the one who thinks of writing thank-you notes, who calls her friends if they miss school, who makes birthday cards for Grandma. She *always* remembers to hug everyone good-bye.

Hugging. They tell stories of when she was little and always asked for "shoulder"—so sweetly, of course. She walks up to Mom or Dad, even now, and gives them a hug.

I never think of hugging, but she does. So how can I walk up and hug them? They would think I was copying her.

She *is* sweet—even to me. She would help me with just about anything, I guess. And she even hugs *me* when I'm upset about something.

But, Lord, it's hard having a sister who's so sweet and huggy. Everyone notices her instead of me.

Lord, Help Me Love My Sister

When I sit in my room thinking about my sister, I remember all the good times we have had playing together, making things, planning family surprises, going on trips. I think of how many times we've shared our deepest feelings and thoughts.

Sitting in my room now I thank you for my little sister. I realize that a lot of who I am comes from the life we have lived together as sisters.

But when I leave my room, and we start to play a game or clean the family room or try to agree on where to ride our bikes, it's so hard to be good sisters.

Loving is a hard thing, Lord.

Please forgive me. I haven't learned not to be jealous, not to get angry, not to want my own way—and neither has she. Will we ever learn, Lord?

I want my sister to be my friend, but I can't do it without your help. Please help me think of the words to say and the things to do to make our love grow a little more today.

Lord, Help Me Love My Sister

Lord, my sister means so much to me. She's tried to help and teach and mother me ever since I can remember. She has felt much more responsible for me than I have for her. She really has put up with a lot of teasing and tantrums and has given in to me more than she should have.

There is no doubt in my mind that my sister loves me.

But there is probably doubt in hers that I love her.

I don't know why I rebel so much against her advice and help, why I want *her* things, *her* friends, *her* chances to go places.

I really do love her, Lord, but maybe I don't know how to love as you want me to love her. Please forgive me.

I want to be my sister's forever friend, but I make so many mistakes each day. I don't seem to be showing her often enough how much she means to me.

Teach me to love my sister, Lord. Help us both learn more about real friendship from facing together the problems that come up today.

Prayers for My Sister

The following pages are for your prayers and thoughts about your relationship with your own sister. There are portions of Scripture at the top of each page to help start your thinking.

Remember, *whatever* it is that is keeping you and your sister apart *today,* you can share with God. Ask for God's help and you will receive it.

"Love is patient" (1 Corinthians 13:4).

"Love is kind" (1 Corinthians 13:4).

"[Love] envies no one" (1 Corinthians 13:4).

"Love is never boastful, nor conceited"
(1 Corinthians 13:4-5).

"Love is never . . . rude" (1 Corinthians 13:5).

*"Love is . . . never selfish"
(1 Corinthians 13:5).*

*"Love is . . . not quick to take offense"
(1 Corinthians 13:5).*

"Love keeps no score of wrongs"
(1 Corinthians 13:5).

"Love . . . does not gloat over [my sister's] sins, but delights in the truth" (1 Corinthians 13:6).

"There is nothing love cannot face; there is no limit to its faith, its hope, and its endurance"
(1 Corinthians 13:7).

*"Love will never come to an end"
(1 Corinthians 13:8).*

*"There are three things that last for ever:
faith, hope, and love"
(1 Corinthians 13:13).*

"The greatest [thing of] all is love"
(1 Corinthians 13:13).

"Lord, help me love my sister."

The Author

Born in Washington, D.C., Clair Cosby grew up as an only child in that city and its Virginia suburbs. Her father died when she was nine years old; her mother remarried when Clair was twelve. Clair graduated from Mary Washington College in Fredericksburg, Virginia, with a B.A. in English and French. She has completed 30 graduate hours  in the field of learning disabilities from the University of Virginia and James Madison University.

Virginia State Vice-President of the Future Teachers of America in high school, Clair has enjoyed her years in the teaching profession. She has taught educable mentally retarded, learning disabled, and emotionally disturbed students ranging in age from seven through eighteen, and is currently teaching a sixth-grade self-contained E.D./L.D. class in the Fauquier County Schools.

Clair is married to J. Mason Cosby, pastor of the Warrenton United Methodist Church, Warrenton, Virginia. The Cosbys have three children: Sarah, Sallie, and James.

Actively involved in church work all her life, Clair has led and been a member of choirs, church school classes, prayer and missionary groups, and she has established and worked on many church newsletters. Especially enjoying work with the church school, she has developed a series of teaching enrichment seminars for local churches and has taught in children, youth, and adult divisions during the past 20 years.

Clair is looking forward to continuing her writing ministry, sharing the good news of Jesus Christ as an outgrowth of her daily personal adventure with God.